I Wonder
Why It's
Christmas

Esther Ekunola

Dedication

This book is dedicated to the Almighty,
to whom all glory belongs.

'Then the angel said to her "Do not be afraid Mary for you have found favour with God" and behold you will conceive in your womb and bring forth a son and shall call his name Jesus'

Luke 1 vs30-31

Once upon a time, an angel appeared to Mary who *lived in Nazareth, a town in Galilee*. Mary was about to be married to Joseph.

One day, God sent an angel called Gabriel to Mary. He said, "Fear not, thou hast found favour with God. You will have a son and you shall call his name Jesus." The angel said to Mary, "Jesus will be a great king and his kingdom shall last forever". (Luke 1 vs 26-31)

Mary was very surprised; she said to the angel, "How can I have a son? I am not yet married to my *fiancé, Joseph*."

Angel Gabriel replied to Mary, "With God, nothing is impossible. It will be the work of God who can do anything. Your son, Jesus, will be holy and he will be the son of God."

Mary bowed her head. "I am God's servant; I will do what he wants me to do." Mary was obedient and humble to the word of God. She happily received the message from God. When Mary looked up, the angel was gone. And it came to pass, Mary became pregnant.

Joseph was a kind man, but when he heard that Mary was expecting a baby, he thought it was not right for him to marry her. That night, he had a dream that an angel told him that he should marry Mary and that her son was the son of God. He would be called Jesus and he would save people from God's punishment for the bad things they had done.

The next day, Joseph remembered what the angel had told him. He accepted Mary and made arrangements for the wedding and soon they were married. Joseph promised to take care of Mary and her son.

What animal is Mary riding on?

4

Joseph now went to Judea, into the city of David which is called Bethlehem, as Joseph was from the lineage of David. Joseph went with his pregnant wife, Mary. It was late when they reached Bethlehem and Mary was tired. Joseph tried to find a room to stay in for the night but everywhere was already occupied. He walked through the cold dark streets, leading the donkey which Mary rode on.

Can you spot Joseph's cloak?

Joseph led the donkey to the stable. He helped Mary down. He then made a soft bed of straw for her on the floor and covered it with his cloak. Mary was thankful that she could rest at last.

That night, Mary gave birth to baby Jesus. She washed him and wrapped him in the clothes she had brought with her. Joseph filled a manger with soft, clean silage to make a bed for the baby and Mary laid him gently in it. Mary called her new baby Jesus, just as the angel had told her.

How many stars can you spot in the sky?

In the same city, which is Bethlehem, there were shepherds abiding in the field, keeping watch over their flocks by night.

The angel of the Lord stood in front of them. They were so frightened, so the angel said to them, "Do not be afraid; I have wonderful news for you and for all people. Tonight, the son of God was born in a stable in Bethlehem. Go now; you shall see a sign unto you and find a baby wrapped in swaddling clothes."

How many stars can you spot in the sky?

As the shepherds looked at the angel, more angels appeared in the sky, singing praises to God; "Glory to God in the highest and on earth, peace and goodwill toward men". Then the angels disappeared and it became dark again.

The shepherds were excited and said to one another, "Let us now quickly go to Bethlehem and look for this child". They agreed and gathered up their things in a hurry to go to the little town of Bethlehem.

What is the name of Mary and Joseph's Son?

The shepherds found the stable and knocked on the door, then they crept quietly in. They looked at the baby lying in a manger and knelt down in front of him and told Joseph and Mary what the angel had said to them.

Afterwards, the shepherds strode through the streets and told everyone about the good news that the son of God had been born that night, and soon, the news of the birth of Jesus spread like a wildfire throughout the whole town.

The shepherds were singing praises to God and went back to their sheep on the hills outside Bethlehem.

In the quiet stable, Mary looked at baby Jesus and thought about the shepherds and what the angel had told them. She wondered about it in her mind.

On the eighth day, baby Jesus was circumcised according to Jewish custom and he was given the name Jesus.

Jesus was born to the world as a gift by God to save mankind. His purpose was to save the world from all our sins. 'For God so love the world that he gave His only begotten son.' [scriptures John 3 vs 16] God showed us his love through his son because God is love. God loved the world so much, especially mankind. He did not want Satan to deceive us anymore like he had done to Adam and Eve in the garden of Eden. God then gave us his son to be born and die for our sins so that Jesus could bring us back to God. Jesus, through his obedient teaching, taught us the true way that God wants us to behave. Finally, he died for us on the cross at Calvary, that is why Jesus is our saviour.

How many wise men can you find?

In a city far from Bethlehem lived some wise men who studied the stars. They saw a new star which was much brighter than all other stars. They knew it must mean something special had happened. After they had studied the star, they decided that it meant a new ruler had been born and they must go and find him.

The three shepherds took presents for this new ruler and followed the star which moved across the night sky ahead of them. At last, they arrived in Jerusalem. They said, "We have seen his star in the sky and know he is born to be the king of the Jews".

When King Herod, who was king at the time in Jerusalem, heard that three strangers were trying to find the new king, baby Jesus, who had been born, he was angry and frightened.

The Roman ruler had made Herod the king of the Jews. Herod asked his priests and other wise men about the new-born king, baby Jesus. They studied the old records and told King Herod that many years ago, it had been forecast that the King of the Jews would be born in Bethlehem.

Herod spoke to the wise men when they came. He told them to go to Bethlehem and when they found baby Jesus, they should let him know so that he could worship him too. The wise men agreed and started their journey to Bethlehem. The star moved ahead of them and stopped at the town of Bethlehem. The wise men knew that they had come to the right place.

They found out where Joseph and Mary were. When they saw baby Jesus, the wise men knelt down in front of him and gave him the presents they had brought with them.

Can you spot baby Jesus' gifts?

The presents were gold, frankincense and myrrh. Then the wise men went quietly away.

On their way back to King Herod in Jerusalem, they camped outside Bethlehem. They had a dream that night in which the angel of the Lord warned them that they must not return to King Herod in Jerusalem.

The angel revealed to the wise men that King Herod planned to kill baby Jesus. In the morning, they loaded their camels and went a different way back to their own country.

How many soldiers can you count?

22

Joseph also had a dream; an angel warned him that baby Jesus was in danger and he must take Mary and the baby to Egypt where they would be safe. Quickly, Joseph, Mary and baby Jesus started their journey to Egypt while it was dark.

When Herod realised that the wise men had tricked him, he was furious and afraid that the new king would take his throne. He ordered his soldiers to march to Bethlehem and kill all boys under the age of two years old.

The people had always hated this cruel king and now they hated him more for killing children under the age of two.

Mary and Joseph lived safely in Egypt with baby Jesus. Then, Joseph had another dream. An angel told him that King Herod was dead and he should take Mary and baby Jesus back to Nazareth.

Mary and Joseph obeyed and took baby Jesus to settle back in Nazareth.

Christians celebrate Christmas because of the birth of Jesus. This is to remind all

Christians that Jesus was born to save the world and to die for all our sins. So, we rejoice in the season for what Jesus has done for us. God said in the Bible, "whosoever believes that Jesus Christ was born to save the world and does not have doubt in his mind shall be saved." (Mark 16 vs 31)

This season is about Jesus.

Merry Christmas.

QUESTIONS

1. Which town did Mary live in when the angel appeared to her?

2. How many wise men gave gifts to baby Jesus?

3. Name the gifts given to Jesus.

4. In which town was Jesus born and where?

5. What is the name of the king that wanted to kill Jesus?

6. What is the name of the angel that appeared to Mary?

7. What is the name of Mary's fiancé?

8. Why do Christians celebrate Christmas?

9. Which country was Jesus taken to for safety?

10. What made the shepherds frightened?

Printed in Great Britain
by Amazon